D1622333

SOUL SURFER

STUDY GUIDE

SOUL SURFER

STUDY GUIDE

FEATURES FAITH-BASED MATERIALS
FOR CHURCH GROUPS, FAMILIES, AND INDIVIDUALS

Published by Outreach, Inc. in partnership with TriStar Pictures.

Outreach Inc., Vista CA 92081

Outreach.com

All scripture quotations, unless otherwise indicated, are taken from the Holy Bible, New International Version®, NIV®. Copyright © 1973, 1978, 1984 by Biblica, Inc.™ Used by permission of Zondervan. All rights reserved worldwide.

Scripture taken from The Message. Copyright © 1993, 1994, 1995, 1996, 2000, 2001, 2002. Used by permission of NavPress Publishing Group.

Scripture taken from the New Century Version. Copyright © 2005 by Thomas Nelson, Inc. Used by permission. All rights reserved.

ISBN: 978-1-9355-4145-5

Cover and interior design: Alexia Wuerdeman and Tim Downs
Heart of A Soul Surfer Photography: noahhamiltonphoto.com

Printed in the United States of America

TABLE OF CONTENTS

INTRODUCTION

Chronicling the rise of a promising young athlete, a debilitating tragedy,and one of the greatest sports comebacks ever, *SOUL SURFER* is a poignant story about the heart and soul of a champion, Bethany Hamilton. By age thirteen the Hawaiian native was well respected in the surfing world, but her dream of becoming a pro surfer was interrupted on October 31, 2003, when she was attacked by a fourteen-foot tiger shark while surfing off Kauai's North Shore.

Losing more than half her blood, yet miraculously surviving, Bethany was now living without a left arm. The determination to pursue her dream, however, had not been taken away. She was back in the water three weeks later, learning to paddle with one arm and to find her balance on the surfboard. She has gone on to win several surfing titles, reaching the top twelve in the Association of Surfing Professionals world rankings in 2009.

Bethany Hamilton has become an inspiration to people around the world, transcending the sport of surfing by overcoming adversity, achieving her dreams, and encouraging others to do the same.

The Campaign

We're pleased you've chosen this four-week *SOUL SURFER* DVD-based Study. It is a good choice for you, your family, your adult small group, your youth group, or a group of families with teens and young children. The *SOUL SURFER* DVD-based Study offers practical, biblical teaching that will help you build a strong relationship with God, enable you to discover His purpose for your life, and help you persevere even in the midst of unexpected tragedies and disappointments.

> *"For I know the plans I have for you," declares the LORD, "plans to prosper you and not to harm you, plans to give you hope and a future."* —Jeremiah 29:11

This four-week DVD-based Study features *Heart of a Soul Surfer*—an inspiring thirty-minute documentary with exclusive surfing and family footage of Bethany Hamilton before and after the shark attack. *Heart of a Soul Surfer* digs deep into the heart of Bethany's unwavering faith in God and provides video clips to support the four lessons in this study. Anyone who has struggled with loss will find that this study and the documentary clips present a story of hope and overcoming life's heartbreaks.

Bethany challenges us, *"I had a choice to make and it was to either follow God or give up on life. I chose to follow God and so much good has come through that ... and through this whole ordeal. And I'm challenging you to choose whether you are going to give up on life or give God a chance ... and let Him work through you."* For all of us, *SOUL SURFER* is a story of faith in God and living for His purposes. This study will challenge and touch the lives of everyone.

Four *SOUL SURFER* lessons will help you:

- Gain Perspective
- Exhibit Perseverance
- Stay Positive
- Discover Purpose

Heart of a Soul Surfer, the Documentary

Bethany Hamilton is a young teen surfer from Kauai, Hawaii, who lost her arm in a shark attack. *Heart of a Soul Surfer* tells her story from early childhood to the shark attack and then through her recovery. The documentary also follows Bethany as she works to understand what her life is going to look like now that her dream of becoming a professional surfer seems to have been lost along with her arm. Bethany's story reveals a strong, loving family, devoted friendships, and an unwavering faith in God. After the shark attack, the documentary follows Bethany through her recovery, coming to grips with her losses, and what it all means for the rest of her life.

The video clips from the documentary will give you insights into Bethany's deeply committed relationship with Jesus Christ, her profound desire to understand God's purpose for her, and her determination to live according to that purpose.

Lesson Two of the DVD-based Study includes a video clip that addresses the shark attack. You will notice there is a Parents' Advisory in that section. The clip is not graphic; the screen focus is underwater as if looking up toward the surfboard and the light sky. There is no actual shark-attack scene. We see Bethany's friends sharing and hear her voice-over describing what happened. Although the clip is not graphic, it might be disturbing for young children. During this section, leaders and parents should use discretion if there are young children participating in the study.

SOUL SURFER, the Movie

SOUL SURFER is the inspiring true story of teen surfer Bethany Hamilton, who lost her arm in a shark attack and courageously overcame all odds to become a champion again, inspiring millions worldwide through the love of her family, her sheer determination, and unwavering faith. The film features an all-star cast, including AnnaSophia Robb and Helen Hunt, with Carrie Underwood in her film debut and Dennis Quaid.

This Study Guide includes references to scenes in SOUL SURFER, and we recommend you watch the scenes as you go through your study. There are two ways you can watch the SOUL SURFER movie scenes:

1. The SOUL SURFER DVD-based Study has instructions on how to view the clips online.

2. If you have the SOUL SURFER movie DVD (available mid 2011), you can find the scenes based on their descriptions in this guide.

USING THIS CURRICULUM

The *SOUL SURFER* DVD-based Study is designed for use by adult groups, families, youth groups, or intergenerational groups that include teens and younger children in their meetings. It also works well for individuals, although you might want to save the games and activities for when you're with friends or family.

You will need the following materials to conduct a *SOUL SURFER* group:

- One *SOUL SURFER* Leader's Guide for the group leader or parent
- One *SOUL SURFER* Resource DVD to show the weekly video clips from the *Heart of a Soul Surfer* documentary
- One *SOUL SURFER* Resource CD containing the activity sheets and instructions for the weekly Paddling Out exercise
- *SOUL SURFER* Study Guides, one for every adult and teen participant

Curriculum Format

The *SOUL SURFER* lessons are organized in sections. Each section is described below. The sections intended for adults, teens, and younger children are clearly identified. In keeping with the surfing theme, we have chosen some section titles that reflect "surf speak."

PRAYER

We recommend that you open and close each lesson with prayer.

 ### CHECKING THE WAVES

Group participants may complete the Checking the Waves section before or during your study. This section introduces you to the lesson topic and helps you evaluate where you stand on the subject before entering into your discussion.

MEMORY VERSE

Each week, you have a verse to memorize. Some in your group may choose to simply read the verse; others will commit to memorizing it. The importance of Bible memorization is that God will use the verses you have memorized to help, guide, and encourage you long after you conclude this study.

 ### PADDLING OUT

To get the group engaged, each week's lesson includes an activity. The Paddling Out section offers a more active option for kinesthetic learners (those of you who learn through moving, doing, touching). Note: The Paddling Out section is optional. You may skip it if you have a limited amount of time, but, we encourage you to try this section at least once. Paddling Out is designed to add to the fun and to help illustrate the principles for the week's lesson. So, check it out!

THE FILMS

The **SOUL SURFER** Resource DVD contains clips from *Heart of a Soul Surfer*, the documentary about Bethany Hamilton's life. The lesson includes instructions as to when to watch each clip and discuss your observations.

We also recommend that you watch scenes from the film **SOUL SURFER**. The Films section will describe one or more scenes from the movie, and you can watch them when you're able. The **SOUL SURFER** Leader's Guide in the DVD-based Study Kit has instructions for watching movie clips online. If you have access to the Internet during your group study, or if you have a **SOUL SURFER** movie DVD, watch the scene(s) as you go through the weekly lesson.

THE DISCUSSION

The Discussion section should be the main portion of your meeting each week. You will find discussion sections after each of the documentary clips and also after The Illustration. We also include discussion questions based on selected Bible passages to support the principles addressed in each lesson.

THE ILLUSTRATION

The Illustration section includes a modern-day story or a biblical example as an illustration of each week's lesson. Have group members read The Illustration beforehand, or read it together during your meeting.

THE REFLECTION

This section contains three questions that will help you draw some conclusions about the lesson's teaching and how it applies to your life. You can answer one Reflection question—or do all three. Don't skip over this section or treat it lightly. It is in the reflection and application to our lives that the principles of each lesson gain power to transform, and transformation is what the study of the Bible is all about.

Guidelines for Adult and Teen Groups

Small groups can have an enormous impact on your life and faith. They help you build friendships and provide support, and they offer you a close group of people who can encourage you and hold you accountable for personal and spiritual growth. The guidelines below will establish expectations and help you get the most from your time together.

- **Confidentiality:** Remember that everything shared in your group should be considered confidential unless you are given specific permission to share it elsewhere. Confidentiality protects your group and creates a safe place of support and acceptance for everyone.

- **Openness:** Do your best to be open and honest during discussions. Your transparency will encourage others to do the same.

- **Respect:** Everyone has the right to an opinion. All questions should be encouraged and answered in a courteous manner. Listen attentively to others without interrupting and be slow to judge. Be careful with sentences that start with, "You should ..." or, "You ought ..." and try not to give advice unless you're asked.

- **Priority:** Make the small group meeting a priority in your schedule. If you're unable to attend or are running late, call your group leader.

- **Preparedness:** If your group decides to do portions of the lesson ahead of time, such as the Checking the Waves section or reading The Illustration before coming to the meeting, prepare your lesson and come ready to share. What you put into the lesson is what you'll get out of it!

- **Participation:** Participate in the discussion but keep your answers brief enough that others can share as well. The principle of participation says, "If there are ten people in the group, share slightly less than one-tenth of the time. If there are eight, share slightly less than one-eighth," etc.

- **Honesty:** When appropriate, thoughtfully offer suggestions to the leader to improve the study.

- **Connection:** Seek to know and care for other group members, as well as share with transparency your emotional, spiritual, and physical needs.

- **Care:** If a member misses a meeting, be sure someone in the group calls to see how they're doing and catch them up on what was missed.

- **Support:** Actively support these guidelines and any other goals and values your group agrees to. Support your leaders and make their job easier by following their directions. Successful groups don't have to agree on every point, but they do agree to disagree sometimes. Refrain from gossip and criticism; if you have concerns or questions about a member's views or statements, communicate directly with that person.

Guidelines for Groups with Children

All of the guidelines for adult groups apply to groups that include children. In addition, here are a few other considerations:

- **Sequence of questions:** When a children's question is included in the lesson, it is often a good idea to ask that question before having the adults answer their version of the question. Asking the children to respond first gives them a chance to share their insights without feeling like the adults have already given all of the possible answers.

- **Age appropriateness:** Although openness and transparency are always valued in group discussions, be considerate of the younger children in the group. Limit your discussion to topics that are age appropriate, and be aware of your vocabulary so that it doesn't exclude the children from understanding the conversation.

- **Pace:** Keep the study moving. Be careful not to allow a discussion of one topic to go on too long, and don't let too much time go by without directing a question to the children in the group.

- **Honor:** Treat the younger members of the group with as much honor as the older ones. Ask for their opinions on issues and value their input and contributions. Children will know if you are patronizing them, though, so be genuine!

- **Encouragement:** Participating as equal contributors in a group with adults is a valuable experience for children. Encourage the young people to contribute and affirm them for their participation. They should experience both spiritual and social growth as a result of being a part of this intergenerational study.

LESSON ONE

Searching for Something Bigger

GAIN A GREATER PERSPECTIVE BY UNDERSTANDING GOD'S PLANS AND PURPOSES.

SEARCHING FOR SOMETHING BIGGER

An experienced surfer has a perspective on the surf conditions that people who don't surf cannot see or understand. Surfers sit on their boards out in the ocean and watch the horizon—waiting for something bigger than their last ride. The swells slowly build until they reach a peak and begin to peel in one or both directions; this is the moment that the fun begins for a surfer. Then, it is experience that gives a surfer the necessary perspective to read the wave and decide if it is the right one to catch.

God's plans, like the waves in the ocean, are more easily seen and understood by people who build up experience. Those who are dedicated to following God and accustomed to listening to Him and His Word are more likely to read "God waves." This ability to discern God's plans and purposes is not, however, out of our reach, nor is it reserved for only a sacred few. God longs to give us the desires of our hearts, and fulfilling God's purpose for our lives is what brings true happiness. Bethany understood that even surfing could not be more important to her than her relationship with God and His plans for her. Bethany yearned for *something bigger*—something only God could create.

The Bible makes it clear that God has a good plan and purpose for our lives (Jeremiah 29:11). The Bible also tells us that God who created the universe knows each one of us intimately (Psalm 139). He knew each of us before we were born. He knows the number of hairs on our heads and everything about our daily lives (Matthew 10:29-31). He knows when we are ready for something bigger! Not only does God love us, He has good plans for us, bigger plans than we can imagine. He has the big picture, the perspective to see what we cannot see. He is waiting for each of us to be ready to trust Him and jump into something bigger.

In this week's lesson, we're going to study biblical principles that will help us learn how to really understand God's purposes and plans for us. Just as Bethany moved from searching for bigger rides in the ocean to searching for a purpose bigger than surfing, we too can search for something bigger. God's purposes and plans for our lives are bigger than anything we can dream up.

CHECKING THE WAVES

This Activity Is for Adults and Teens

Each week, the *Checking the Waves* activity will give you a feel for where you are before the session begins. For example, this week you're going to consider how well you react or respond when unexpected difficulties hit your life or the lives of loved ones. When you finish each week's lesson, come back to Checking the Waves and look at your answers. You might find that the *Paddling Out* activity, the Bible verses, or the discussion has given you a different perspective.

Before you begin this week's group or family discussion, rate your level of agreement with the following statements about God's perspective and plans for you and your ability to accept them.

1. I am confident that God has a good and specific purpose for my life.

___ Strongly Agree ___ Agree ___ Neutral ___ Disagree __ Strongly Disagree

2. I believe that God's purpose for my life is bigger and more exciting than I can imagine.

___ Strongly Agree ___ Agree ___ Neutral ___ Disagree __ Strongly Disagree

3. I believe God's promises strongly enough to obey and do what He asks, even when I do not have a clear idea how things will turn out.

___ Strongly Agree ___ Agree ___ Neutral ___ Disagree __ Strongly Disagree

4. I believe God will be faithful to His future plans for me, even when my current circumstances are confusing.

___ Strongly Agree ___ Agree ___ Neutral ___ Disagree __ Strongly Disagree

5. I believe God can accomplish good things in my life through circumstances as difficult as family issues, financial struggles, medical problems, accidents, or even death.

___ Strongly Agree ___ Agree ___ Neutral ___ Disagree __ Strongly Disagree

6. I believe my faith is strong enough to survive God's testing of my trust in Him.

___ Strongly Agree ___ Agree ___ Neutral ___ Disagree __ Strongly Disagree

7. I believe that if I could see my circumstances from God's perspective, everything would make sense.

___ Strongly Agree ___ Agree ___ Neutral ___ Disagree __ Strongly Disagree

QUESTION 1: Which of these statements caused you to think the longest before answering? Why?

_____

_____

_____

_____

THIS WEEK'S MEMORY VERSE:

"For I know the plans I have for you," declares the LORD, "plans to prosper you and not to harm you, plans to give you hope and a future." —Jeremiah 29:11

Memorizing verses from the Bible is the best way to recall the reasons why we can trust God when the circumstances in life are not easy. The more Scripture you have committed to memory, the more the Holy Spirit can guide you, encourage you, and comfort you.

PRAYER: Open in prayer.

PADDLING OUT: THE LINE OR THE DOT?

Object Lesson for Adults, Teens, and Children

This object lesson uses a simple illustration to help us visualize how our perspective compares with God's bigger perspective.

LEADER/PARENT: Find the instructions for setting up the object lesson and the script for teaching "The Line or the Dot?" in the Lesson One folder on your *SOUL SURFER* Resource CD.

THE DOCUMENTARY

If you have not yet seen the documentary *Heart of a Soul Surfer*, read the brief description below. Interestingly, Bethany's older brother Noah, who is now a professional photographer and videographer, has had a filmmaking hobby since Bethany was a baby. As a result, this documentary is not made up of reenactments, but of actual footage of Bethany throughout her life.

Heart of a Soul Surfer is the true story of Bethany Hamilton, a competitive young surfer who grew up in Kauai, Hawaii. As Bethany relaxed on her board along with her friends waiting for the next wave on October 31, 2003, she was attacked by a shark. The shark took her left arm, but her friends were able to get her a quarter mile back to the shore and summon an ambulance to take her to the hospital.

Before the attack, Bethany was a committed Christian who desired above all else to understand God's purpose and plan for how He wanted her to live her life. When she realized what had happened to her, she prayed for God to help her. While she was still in the hospital, she was already aware that God was answering her prayers and that even this loss was part of His plan to use her for His purposes. Although her dream of being a professional surfer appeared to be finished, she still trusted God to make His purpose clear.

Within three weeks of the attack, Bethany was back in the water, determined to surf again. Six months later she was competing in the National Scholastic Surfing Association Nationals and won. Bethany's story has inspired millions around the world with her perseverance and unwavering faith in Jesus Christ's good plan for her life. When asked how she could be so confident that God would use this tragedy, she quotes Romans 8:28: "In all things God works for the good of those who love him, who have been called according to his purpose."

Watch the first Lesson One video clip on the *SOUL SURFER* Resource DVD.

God, Please Use Me: This clip helps us understand the kind of child Bethany was and her love for God as she grew up. By the age of thirteen, she not only knew she wanted to be a professional surfer, she also realized that what was most important to her was to discover God's purpose for her life. Interestingly, two weeks before the shark attack, Bethany and her mother began praying in earnest about God's will for her life.

LEADER/PARENT TIP: Where a children's question is included in the lesson, it is often a good idea to ask that question before having the adults answer their version of the question. Asking the children to respond first gives them a chance to share their insights without feeling like the adults have already given all of the possible answers.

QUESTION 2: Even as a little girl, Bethany Hamilton seemed to be "searching for something bigger," as our study this week is entitled. Why do you suppose she was so spiritually sensitive at such a young age?

Alternate wording for younger children: Why do you think Bethany loved Jesus so much when she was just a little girl?

Read Isaiah 49:1b.

> **Before I was born the LORD called me; from my birth he has made mention of my name.** —Isaiah 49:1b

QUESTION 3: God's plans for us are not afterthoughts; He doesn't make up a plan for us as our lives go along. Based on Isaiah 49:1b, when was Isaiah called by God to do His work? What does this verse suggest about God's plans for your life?

Alternate wording for younger children: This verse tells us that God made plans for Isaiah to tell people what God wanted them to know. When did God first decide that He would use Isaiah to talk to the people?

THE FILMS

Watch the second Lesson One video clip on the *SOUL SURFER* Resource DVD.

Hospital: This footage was filmed during the first days that Bethany was in the hospital after the shark attack. We are able to see just what is so remarkable about this young lady when she is lying in the hospital bed, freshly bandaged, and says that the reason she might have been bitten by the shark is "so I can tell others about God and help them go to heaven." We are also introduced to her youth pastor, Sarah Hill, who first gave her the Bible promise that is today's memory verse, Jeremiah 29:11.

THE DISCUSSION

QUESTION 4: Thinking back on our object lesson about perspective in the Paddling Out section, how did Bethany demonstrate that she was looking at the shark attack from God's perspective? What might she have said differently if she was looking at it from a human perspective?

Alternate wording for younger children: Do you think Bethany knew that God sees things in our lives differently than we do? How do you think that helped her when she was in the hospital?

THE FILMS

Watch the *SOUL SURFER* movie scene in which Sarah teaches the youth group.

LEADER/PARENT: See the *SOUL SURFER* Leader's Guide for information on how to watch scenes from the movie *SOUL SURFER*.

A group of teenagers, including Bethany, are gathered in the church's beachfront hall for the youth group "RAD Nite." Youth leader Sarah Hill leads them in a game she calls "Can You Tell Your Ear from Your Elbow?" during which the teens look at zoomed-in pictures, such as a fly's eye and a walnut, and have to guess what they're seeing. Sarah uses the strange pictures to make an important point—that frequently the best way to make sense of life is to step back, see a different point of view, and "get some perspective."

SOUL SURFER Quote

"So, if you're dealing with something that's hard to handle or just plain doesn't make sense, do whatever it takes to get some perspective. Talk to your parents, come see me, or pray about it. From a different point of view, you'll often discover that things aren't quite as confusing as they seem."

— Sarah to the youth group

THE DISCUSSION

Read the memory verse: Jeremiah 29:11.

> **"For I know the plans I have for you," declares the LORD, "plans to prosper you and not to harm you, plans to give you hope and a future".** —Jeremiah 29:11

In this passage, God is speaking to the people of Israel through the prophet Jeremiah. The Israelites are about to be conquered by their enemies, the Babylonians, and spend the next seventy years in exile. But God reassures His people that they will return home to Israel, and He will listen to them and bless them.

QUESTION 5: When youth leader Sarah Hill shared this verse with Bethany, how do you think the verse helped Bethany deal with the shark attack and losing her arm?

Now, read Jeremiah 29:11 in its context. The Israelites are about to be conquered by their enemies as a consequence of their repeated disobedience. Yet God's gracious message to them as they face seventy years in exile is, "I will take care of you."

This is what the LORD says: "When seventy years are completed for Babylon, I will come to you and fulfill my gracious promise to bring you back to this place. For I know the plans I have for you," declares the LORD, "plans to prosper you and not to harm you, plans to give you hope and a future. Then you will call upon me and come and pray to me, and I will listen to you. You will seek me and find me when you seek me with all your heart. I will be found by you," declares the LORD, "and will bring you back from captivity. I will gather you from all the nations and places where I have banished you," declares the LORD, "and will bring you back to the place from which I carried you into exile." —Jeremiah 29:10-14

QUESTION 6: According to Jeremiah 29:11, what is God's message to us when life is most dark? God makes some promises in verses 12 and 14; what did the Israelites need to do to claim those promises? What meaning do these promises have for us today?

Alternate wording for younger children: When God says He won't abandon you, He means He won't ever leave you. What things in Jeremiah 29:11 do you think helped Bethany after the shark attacked her?

Read the following section—either quietly to yourself as you prepare for your weekly session or aloud during the discussion time with your group or family. The Illustration for each lesson will feature a real-life example or a Bible story that will help you understand and apply each lesson.

The book of Ruth opens with Naomi and her husband, Elimelech, living in Bethlehem, in the land God had promised to the Israelites. At that time the people had no king, but they had judges to help keep them safe from other nations. When we first see Naomi and Elimelech, there is a famine in the land, so they take their two sons and move to Moab. Moab was a nation that did not know the true God of Israel but worshiped pagan gods. After they live in Moab for some time, Elimelech dies. Both of Naomi's sons had married Moabite women, and at some point both of Naomi's sons also die. In those days widowed women relied on their sons to provide for them, but now Naomi and her daughters-in-law, Ruth and Orpah, find themselves without support or financial security.

Naomi hears that the famine in Bethlehem has lifted, so she, Ruth, and Orpah start out for her homeland. They haven't gone far when Naomi has second thoughts, and tells her daughters-in-law to return to their families in Moab because they will have no hope of marrying in Bethlehem. Orpah returns, but Ruth insists on staying with Naomi and seeing to her needs.

Once they arrive in Bethlehem, they have no one to help them financially. Naomi becomes bitter and unhappy with the way she perceives God has dealt with her, but Ruth does her best to provide and do as Naomi instructs. Ruth goes to the fields and follows the harvesters to pick up the dropped heads of grain in hopes of providing food for herself and her mother-in-law. A man named Boaz owns the field in which she is gleaning, and the story ends happily with Boaz and Ruth marrying.

At the beginning of this story, we could see nothing but tragedy and hopelessness in the lives of both Naomi and Ruth. They had both lost husbands, Naomi had lost both of her children, and neither of them had any means of financial support or security for their future. Their outlook was grim at best.

But God had something bigger in mind—a plan greater than anything either of them could have imagined. God provided a husband for Ruth, yes, and he took care of Ruth and Naomi's physical needs for the rest of their lives. But years later, in a generation they would never live to see, Jesus Christ, the Savior of the world, was born to one of their descendents. If you are intrigued by the story of Naomi, Ruth, and Boaz, you might enjoy reading more about them in the book of Ruth, found in the Bible's Old Testament.

Naomi and Ruth had no idea of the plans God had for them. But without the tragedies of famine, death, and financial loss, neither of them could have fulfilled God's bigger purposes and plan for their lives.

THE DISCUSSION

Read Isaiah 55:8-9.

> *"For my thoughts are not your thoughts, neither are your ways my ways," declares the LORD. "As the heavens are higher than the earth, so are my ways higher than your ways and my thoughts than your thoughts."* —Isaiah 55:8-9

QUESTION 7: If you were talking to Naomi at her most bitter or Ruth in her darkest moments, how would you use these verses to encourage them? What do these verses tell you about the importance of perspective when difficult and unwanted situations occur in your life?

Alternate wording for younger children: God can see things that we can't see, so He allows things in our lives that we don't always understand. When you get the most frustrated, how would it help if you could see what God sees?

Read Proverbs 3:5-6.

> *Trust in the LORD with all your heart and lean not on your own understanding; in all your ways acknowledge him, and he will make your paths straight.* —Proverbs 3:5-6

QUESTION 8: When you're faced with problems or a difficult decision, do you trust in God completely, or do you tend to rely on your own judgment? What would help you lean more on God and His wisdom?

Alternate wording for younger children: To acknowledge God means to believe that He is real and then live like you believe it. To trust Him with all our hearts means that we don't doubt that He will answer our prayers, even if He answers with "No" or "Not yet." What do you need God to do for you? Have you asked Him to help you? Ask Him now and expect Him to show you the answer in bigger ways than you ever thought He would.

From the genealogy of Jesus in Matthew 1:1-16, notice verses 5 and 16:

> **Salmon the father of Boaz, whose mother was Rahab, Boaz the father of Obed, whose mother was Ruth.** —Matthew 1:5

> **and Jacob the father of Joseph, the husband of Mary, of whom was born Jesus, who is called Christ.** —Matthew 1:16

QUESTION 9: In what ways did the tragedies and hardships Naomi and Ruth experienced bring about good that was beyond their understanding?

Alternate wording for younger children: *What do you think made Naomi the happiest about Ruth marrying Boaz?*

FUN FACT:

Naomi and Ruth never expected God was giving them something more than just a husband and someone to provide food, clothing, and a place to live. They didn't know that a child Ruth would have with Boaz would be the grandfather of King David and the ancestor of Jesus.

Read Ephesians 2:10.

For we are God's workmanship, created in Christ Jesus to do good works, which God prepared in advance for us to do.
—Ephesians 2:10

QUESTION 10: As Bethany became convinced that God had good plans for her, she understood that God was going to use her even though she didn't know how or what that might mean. In what ways does Ephesians 2:10 help us feel confident about what God has planned for us?

Alternate wording for younger children: What are some of the good works God wants us to do?

Heart of a Soul Surfer Quote:

Sarah Hill, youth pastor: "The Lord began to show to my heart that Bethany had been a light in a dark industry [surfing], and the Lord was going to now use her as a voice in that industry."

QUESTION 11: What good things have come from the shark's attack on Bethany? In what ways did Bethany use the loss of her arm as a way to "do good works" for others? What could you do to use your difficult circumstances to positively impact the lives of the people around you?

Alternate wording for younger children: How do you think Bethany can help other people since she lost her arm?

THE REFLECTION

Pick one of the three questions below. Take a few moments and think carefully about the question before you answer.

- **What was the most important lesson you learned from this week's lesson?**

- **In the Checking the Waves section, in which area did you strongly disagree or disagree with the statement? Why did you answer that way? What have you learned that can help you grow in that area?**

- **How do you intend to practice seeing things from God's perspective over the next three weeks?**

TIP FOR SUCCESS:

Try pairing up with someone else in your group and asking them to be your accountability partner for the four weeks of the study. As accountability partners, you can help each other keep the commitments you make during the Reflection section of the lesson. Accountability partners should be of the same gender, and from different families.

REFLECTION QUESTION: God wants to give us something bigger than what we understand right now. As we study the Bible, He gives us understanding and perspective about His ways. But God wants to do something bigger in our lives than just giving us knowledge; He wants to transform us to be more like Him. Begin with a little self-evaluation by using the questions below to rate yourself. Choose one area where you would like to grow. In the space provided write out one thing you can begin to do this week to move you in the right direction.

On a scale of 1 to 10, with 10 being highest, rate your life in the following areas:
Rate how your relationship with God is today. (1 is "Not so good" and 10 is "Couldn't be better.")

| 1 | 2 | 3 | 4 | 5 | 6 | 7 | 8 | 9 | 10 | N/A |

Rate how much time you spend in the Bible, in prayer, and listening to God every day. (1 is "very little" and 10 is "I'm connected to God constantly.")

| 1 | 2 | 3 | 4 | 5 | 6 | 7 | 8 | 9 | 10 | N/A |

Rate your expectations when you pray for a miracle. (1 is "I never really expect a positive answer" and 10 is "I would be surprised if God answered no.")

| 1 | 2 | 3 | 4 | 5 | 6 | 7 | 8 | 9 | 10 | N/A |

Write one next step for growth in one of these areas. Share your intended commitment with at least one other person for accountability.

Next Step for Growth: _____

Accountability Partner: _____

Review the Memory Verse: Read the memory verse for this week again (Jeremiah 29:11) and commit it to memory by next week's meeting.

Prayer Requests: Before closing your time together, have each member of your group or family share at least one prayer request.

PRAYER: Close in prayer.

Trusting God in the Impact Zone

LEARN HOW TO KEEP YOUR FAITH STRONG WHEN LIFE GETS TOUGH.

TRUSTING GOD IN THE IMPACT ZONE

To a surfer, the *impact zone* is the place where the waves break the hardest and the most consistently. As each wave crests and then falls, it meets the main body of water and creates an effect almost like that of a powerful washing machine—slamming rough, cold water onto surfers and flipping them around as if they were caught in a spin cycle! The impact zone is definitely not a place to linger; you want to get through it as quickly as possible because it can be a very frightening, disorienting experience to get caught in its vortex. But in order to get in position to catch the waves instead of get pounded by them, every surfer has to paddle **through** the impact zone—there's no way around it, no way to escape. Surfers have to face down that violent cauldron of power every time they want to catch a wave.

The spiritual impact zone is what every soul surfer has to get through before reaching the place where he or she can be the most effective. For each of us, our impact zone is our place of greatest turmoil, darkest confusion, or most intense upset. The faith muscles we develop while facing down and paddling through our spiritual impact zone are the very muscles we need on the other side in order to live out our ultimate purpose. Simply put, it takes trust in God to make it safely through the impact zone. Trusting God in the midst of our chaos develops our faith muscles, which gives us peace even when we don't know the outcome and confidence that God will show up and take care of us.

In this lesson, we're going to see how Bethany handled her impact zone: the shark attack, her recovery, and learning to live with only one arm. Just as Bethany trusted God in the impact zones of her life, we too can learn to trust God when life gets tough.

CHECKING THE WAVES

This Activity Is for Adults and Teens

This week, in the *Checking the Waves* activity, we are going to identify what's in our impact zone. Remember: The impact zone is the place of maximum distress, where a spiritual crisis takes place, where you are facing down the things you fear the most. Different things throw different people into that crisis point. What puts you in the impact zone? From the following list, put a ➡ beside the fear-inducing factors that have created an impact zone for you in the past or could put you in the impact zone in the future. Ask yourself these questions to help you identify your impact zone: What do I fear the most? What has the most power over me? What disrupts my peace?

WHAT PUTS YOU IN THE IMPACT ZONE?

❏	**Abuse**	Suffering from habitual maltreatment
❏	**Criticism**	Harsh attack on your performance or character
❏	**Danger**	Being physically harmed
❏	**Death**	Death of a loved one, or facing your own death
❏	**Deprivation**	Lack of basic necessities (food, shelter)
❏	**Failure**	Shame from not achieving what was expected
❏	**Future**	Anxiety about what's coming
❏	**Guilt**	Self-punishment over past mistakes
❏	**Illness**	Sickness or disease or debilitating injury
❏	**Past**	Carrying the burden of a poor upbringing
❏	**Rebellion**	Being in a state of disobedience
❏	**Rejection**	Abandonment by someone you trusted
❏	**Ridicule**	Being mocked for beliefs, behavior, or performance
❏	**Success**	Having to live up to expectations from past success
❏	**Stress**	Overwhelming convergence of duties and expectations
❏	_____	_____

QUESTION 1: It is in the impact zone that we develop the faith muscles for trusting God, and it is faith that gives us confidence and peace, even in the midst of the chaos. If you are ready and feel comfortable sharing, tell your group about a time in your life you would call an impact zone, and describe how you responded during that time.

In this lesson, we will be discovering ways to trust God more when we're in the impact zone.

THIS WEEK'S MEMORY VERSE:

For I am the LORD, your God, who takes hold of your right hand and says to you, Do not fear; I will help you. —Isaiah 41:13

PRAYER: Open in prayer.

PADDLING OUT: DISASTER CHARADES

Game for Adults, Teens, and Children

Play the classic pantomime game to acquaint group members with Bible characters who faced difficult challenges and triumphed with God's help.

LEADER/PARENT: Find instructions and game sheets for "Disaster Charades" in the Lesson Two folder on your **SOUL SURFER** Resource CD. Print out the "Disaster Charades" game sheets before the meeting.

THE FILMS

Watch the first Lesson Two video clip on the *SOUL SURFER* Resource DVD.

Parents' Advisory

Be sure to watch this scene before the meeting to determine whether it is appropriate for the children in your group. The clip shows only scenes of water and color. It is not graphic or gory, but the event is upsetting and could be disturbing for children to watch.

Shark Attack: This clip describes the events of October 31, 2003, Halloween morning. Bethany and her best friend (Alana), Alana's father (Holt), and Alana's brother (Byron) are all surfing at Tunnels Beach. The clip takes us through the shark attack, getting back to shore, and Bethany heading to the hospital with a word of encouragement from a paramedic, who whispered Hebrews 13:5, "I will never leave you nor forsake you," in her ear.

THE DISCUSSION

QUESTION 2: The shark attack and its aftermath were Bethany's impact zone. In the documentary clip we just saw, as well as in the Lesson One footage of Bethany in the hospital, we saw that Bethany was certain that God was with her in the midst of the accident. How did you see Bethany counting on God as she faced the loss of her arm and the possible loss of her surfing career?

Alternate wording for younger children: Why do you think Bethany talked so much about God in the movie?

Read Isaiah 41:13, Joshua 1:5b, and Psalm 46:1.

> *For I am the LORD, your God, who takes hold of your right hand and says to you, Do not fear; I will help you.* —Isaiah 41:13

> *I will never leave you nor forsake you.* —Joshua 1:5b

> *God is our refuge and strength, an ever-present help in trouble.* —Psalm 46:1

QUESTION 3: How do these verses affect your expectation of what will happen when you go to God for help?

Alternate wording for younger children: How do you think God reacts when we ask Him for help?

Read John 14:25-27 and Romans 15:13.

> *"All this I have spoken while still with you. But the Counselor, the Holy Spirit, whom the Father will send in my name, will teach you all things and will remind you of everything I have said to you. Peace I leave with you; my peace I give you. I do not give to you as the world gives. Do not let your hearts be troubled and do not be afraid."* —John 14:25-27

> *May the God of hope fill you with all joy and peace as you trust in him, so that you may overflow with hope by the power of the Holy Spirit.* —Romans 15:13

QUESTION 4: The Holy Spirit dwells in the hearts of all who follow Jesus Christ. What do we receive through the Holy Spirit to help us in the midst of life's difficulties? How can these verses help you when you feel like you are in the impact zone?

Alternate wording for younger children: When you are in trouble, how can John 14:25-27 help you to trust God?

Read John 16:33.

> *"I told you these things so that you can have peace in me. In this world you will have trouble, but be brave! I have defeated the world."* —John 16:33 (NCV)

QUESTION 5: What comfort and encouragement do you find in Jesus' promise in John 16:33? In what ways do you think Jesus has "defeated the world," and what does that mean for your life?

Alternate wording for younger children: What does Jesus say makes it possible for us to be brave when we have trouble?

THE FILMS

Watch the *SOUL SURFER* movie scene in which Bethany goes to visit Sarah after the shark attack.

Soon after the shark attack, Bethany goes to see her youth leader, Sarah Hill. Bethany is struggling to understand why this tragedy has happened in her life and why God has allowed it. She turns to Sarah for comfort and answers.

SOUL SURFER Quote

"I don't know why terrible things happen to us sometimes, but I want to believe that something good's gonna come out of this. I don't know what it is right now. I wish I did."

— Sarah to Bethany

Read Romans 8:28.

And we know that in all things God works for the good of those who love him, who have been called according to his purpose.
—Romans 8:28

QUESTION 6: From what you read in Romans 8:28, why do you think Sarah was so confident that something good could come out of Bethany's loss?

Alternate wording for younger children: Do you think Bethany felt better after talking to Sarah? Why do you think that?

QUESTION 7: Sometimes the passage of time gives us a better and bigger perspective on life. A number of years have passed since Bethany lost her arm in the shark attack. From what you now know of Bethany's life and impact on others, what good came out of the tragic loss of Bethany's arm?

Alternate wording for younger children: Even though it may seem strange to think that a shark attack could have any good results, see how many good things you can think of that happened because of the shark attack.

THE FILMS

Watch the second Lesson Two video clip on the *SOUL SURFER* Resource DVD.

One Arm, Now What? Even while still in the hospital, Bethany looked remarkably upbeat and positive. But the reality of what she had lost was sinking in. Her friends and family were devastated, yet her father held on to the truth that he was blessed to still have her alive. Bethany begins to think about giving surfing another shot.

Watch the *SOUL SURFER* movie scene in which Bethany wakes up in the hospital and talks with her father.

LEADER/PARENT TIP: See the *SOUL SURFER* Leader's Guide for information on how to watch scenes from the movie *SOUL SURFER*.

Not even forty-eight hours has passed since Bethany lost her arm in a shark attack. She is still in her hospital room, and her father, Tom Hamilton, is keeping a quiet vigil beside her bed. When Bethany awakes, she looks to her father for assurance that she can overcome her tragic loss and get back to the sport she loves. As Tom comforts Bethany, he reminds her of a biblical promise from her Heavenly Father.

SOUL SURFER Quote

Bethany: "When can I surf?"

Tom: "Soon."

Bethany: "How do you know?"

Tom: "Because you 'can do all things ... '"

Bethany: "'... through Him who gives me strength.'"

THE DISCUSSION

Read Psalm 56:3, Philippians 4:11, 13, and Psalm 54:4.

When I am afraid, I will trust in you. —Psalm 56:3

I am not saying this because I am in need, for I have learned to be content whatever the circumstances. ... I can do everything through him who gives me strength. —Philippians 4:11, 13

Surely God is my help; the Lord is the one who sustains me. —Psalm 54:4

QUESTION 8: Often when a great loss like Bethany's occurs, the surrounding family members and friends have just as hard a time accepting the realities of the tragedy. How can these verses help people in the position of Bethany's father or best friend?

Alternate wording for younger children: Why was the shark attack so hard for Bethany's dad and friend?

QUESTION 9: Underline the words or phrases in the verses on the previous pages of this lesson that are most meaningful to you. Which verse encourages you the most? What specifically helps you and why?

Alternate wording for younger children: Is there one word in the verses we've read that helps you? Which verse means the most to you? Why?

_____

_____

_____

_____

_____

THE ILLUSTRATION   *"DADDY, HOLD MY HAND?"*

This story is from the Internet site The Whisper of God. This is a great little story about a little girl who looks to her daddy to comfort and protect her when she is afraid.

I was on a plane yesterday flying to Florida. Behind me sat a father with his two small children. The boy seemed excited to be on the plane and kept looking out the window. He would tell everyone to "look how high we are" and "now we're turning." Being a former "white-knuckled" flier myself, I am sure that his announcements didn't sit too well with some of the people on the plane who just wanted the ride over with and to be back on solid ground again.

But as he made his announcements, his sister just sat between him and her father and never said a word.

I started to fall asleep when I heard this little voice from behind me say, "Dad, I'm scared." Her father told her that there was nothing to be scared about.

She was quiet for another minute or two, and then she said again, "But Dad, I'm scared."

Then in this meek little voice, in which you could hear her anxiety, she both said and asked at the same time, "Daddy? Hold my hand?"

How many times have we been in the same position as this little girl? It doesn't have to be a plane ride that we are scared or worried about. We can be scared or worried about anything at any time; nonetheless, we all have times when we have that little voice inside of us that would like to say, "Hold my hand."

We may no longer have our parents to hold our hands when we are scared. We may now be the person that is asked to hold someone's hand to comfort them. We may need to be strong for others.

No matter how strong we are in our effort to comfort others, there are times when the scared child lives inside of us.

In those times who do we, the strong ones, turn to for our comfort?

We turn to God.

God's own words tell us:

For I am the LORD, your God, who takes hold of your right hand and says to you, Do not fear; I will help you (Isaiah 41:13).

God wants to hold our hand and comfort us. All we need to do is ask for His comfort and then take His hand.

When we got off the plane in Florida, I saw the little girl reach up and take her father's hand again. This time it wasn't for comfort but, rather, as an unspoken, "Thank you, Daddy. I love you."

So, like that little girl, after you have taken God's hand in comfort, take His hand once again to tell Him thank you and that you love Him.[1]

THE DISCUSSION

QUESTION 10: After reading the story about the little girl trusting her daddy to protect and comfort her, think back on Bethany's response right after the shark attack. How was her prayer to God for help similar to the little girl's response when she was afraid on the airplane?

Alternate wording for younger children: Have you ever felt afraid like the little girl on the airplane? How were you able to let go of your fear?

[1] "Daddy? Hold My Hand..." The Whisper of God, accessed December 2010, http://www.thewhisperofgod.com/2009/10/daddy-hold-my-hand/.

QUESTION 11: Where do you turn when you are afraid? Rate yourself below.

Take a couple of minutes to evaluate your reactions to fear. Circle the answer that shows how you usually respond when you are afraid. Just circle one answer for each statement. If none of the answers apply to you (for example, if your parents have passed away), select N/A for Not Applicable.

FOR ADULTS AND TEENS:

When you are afraid:

How often do you turn to your parents?

| Always | Often | Once in a While | Not Often | Never | N/A |

How often do you turn to your spouse?

| Always | Often | Once in a While | Not Often | Never | N/A |

How often do you turn to your friends?

| Always | Often | Once in a While | Not Often | Never | N/A |

How often do you avoid your fear and find something else to focus on?

| Always | Often | Once in a While | Not Often | Never | N/A |

How often do you internalize your fear by worrying?

| Always | Often | Once in a While | Not Often | Never | N/A |

How often do you turn to a destructive habit or addiction for comfort?

| Always | Often | Once in a While | Not Often | Never | N/A |

How often do you turn to the Bible?

| Always | Often | Once in a While | Not Often | Never | N/A |

How often do you turn to God in prayer asking Him for help?

| Always | Often | Once in a While | Not Often | Never | N/A |

Review your answers. Are you satisfied with them? Do you want to make any changes?

_____

_____

_____

_____

_____

Alternate wording for younger children: *Circle one answer for each statement about what you do when you are scared.*

How often do you go to your parents when you are scared?

Always   **Sometimes**   **Never**

How often do you talk to a friend when you are scared?

Always   **Sometimes**   **Never**

How often do you hold your blanket or a stuffed animal when you are scared?

Always   **Sometimes**   **Never**

How often do you run away and hide when you are scared?

Always   **Sometimes**   **Never**

How often do you talk to God when you are scared?

Always   **Sometimes**   **Never**

How often do you read your Bible when you are scared?

Always   **Sometimes**   **Never**

THE REFLECTION

Pick one of the three questions below. Take a few moments and think carefully about the question before you answer.

- What was the most important lesson you learned from this week's lesson?

- Review your answers in the *Checking the Waves* section and then look at how you rated yourself in Question 11. If you are in your impact zone, do you actually respond the way you said you would in Question 11? If your answers are very different, why do you think there is a discrepancy?

- In what ways do you hope to grow stronger when you face an impact zone or another area where you can trust God over the next two weeks?

REFLECTION QUESTION: Read the following verses, and as you read, underline any words that stand out to you or can help you when you enter an impact zone:

> *Let us then approach the throne of grace with confidence, so that we may receive mercy and find grace to help us in our time of need.* —Hebrews 4:16

"Do not let your hearts be troubled. Trust in God; trust also in me." —John 14:1

Praise be to the God and Father of our Lord Jesus Christ, the Father of compassion and the God of all comfort, who comforts us in all our troubles, so that we can comfort those in any trouble with the comfort we ourselves have received from God. For just as the sufferings of Christ flow over into our lives, so also through Christ our comfort overflows. —2 Corinthians 1:3-5

May the God of hope fill you with all joy and peace as you trust in him, so that you may overflow with hope by the power of the Holy Spirit. —Romans 15:13

Go back to the *Checking the Waves* activity and notice which of the fear-inducing factors you indicated would put you into the impact zone. In thinking about your particular impact zone, which verse or verses most apply to you (or appeal to you) when you are faced with that fear or difficult situation? Using the verse or verses as a guide, write down how you will choose to respond when you're in the impact zone:

_____

_____

_____

_____

Commit to applying that verse (or verses) this week, and consider sharing your goal with the group or with someone you trust to hold you accountable.

Review the Memory Verse: Read the memory verse for this week again (Isaiah 41:13) and commit it to memory by next week's meeting.

Prayer Requests: Before closing your time together, have each member of your group or family share at least one prayer request.

PRAYER: Close in prayer.

LESSON THREE

Getting Back in the Water

BE INSPIRED TO PERSEVERE IN THE MIDST OF LIFE'S CHALLENGES.

GETTING BACK IN THE WATER

So far, we have seen Bethany Hamilton demonstrate some amazing character qualities for one so young. In Lesson One we saw that she had already developed an eternal perspective on life, which equipped her ahead of time to handle a crisis. In Lesson Two Bethany showed that in the impact zone, her faith gave her the resilience to survive her many losses and still have hope. Now, we're going to look in on perhaps the greatest test of her character—the aftermath of a tragedy.

Tragedies and hardships expose what we really believe about the goodness of God. "God is good" is a universal belief, yet this commonly held truth comes under fire when it passes through the four stages of a tragedy.

- Stage One: Before a tragedy, we say, "God is good, or so I've always heard."

- Stage Two: During a tragedy, we cry, "God is good, isn't He?"

- Stage Three: After a tragedy, we look back and say, "If God was good, He would have never let that happen."

- Stage Four: Not everyone comes to Stage 4, but at a later time, some arrive at a new belief that says, "God is good, no matter what."

Bethany Hamilton got to Stage Four. In the aftermath of the shark attack, she processed what had happened to her in light of what she knew of God, His promises, and His character. What Bethany concluded was that God was still God, and He had a bigger purpose for her than she had at first believed. Therefore, she determined to push past her doubts and act on her beliefs.

The character quality Bethany demonstrated in the aftermath of the attack was perseverance. Developing perspective before a tragedy hits is crucial. Staying positive in the midst of a tragedy is challenging. But exhibiting perseverance after a tragedy is downright difficult. By getting back in the water on the day before Thanksgiving, Bethany proved to herself and to her family that her God-given dreams were not dead. That was a holy moment that became one of the most inspiring parts of Bethany's story. At first glance, perseverance might not seem like a glamorous quality, but in truth it is the stuff of which heroes are made.

CHECKING THE WAVES

This Activity Is for Adults and Teens

This week in the *Checking the Waves* activity, we are going to see what kinds of things tend to make us feel like quitting. Checking the Waves is a particularly appropriate title for this segment this week, because for a surfer, waves have the potential to be discouraging! Too many waves, not enough waves, violent waves, flat waves—it takes determination, stamina, and perseverance to stick it out and catch the right wave.

What kinds of things discourage you? When you're facing a challenge, whether it's starting a new business, finishing a difficult course, learning a new skill, caring for a troubled friend, or working through a painful relationship, what are the factors that tend to make you want to quit? From this list, check the top three things that are the most likely to make you feel discouraged.

MY TOP-THREE DISCOURAGERS

- ☐ Exhaustion
- ☐ Failure
- ☐ Boredom
- ☐ Poor health
- ☐ Stress
- ☐ Criticism
- ☐ Frustration
- ☐ Rejection
- ☐ Hopeless task
- ☐ Pain
- ☐ Facing multiple problems simultaneously
- ☐ Overcommitted
- ☐ Lack of resources
- ☐ Relational conflict
- ☐ Struggling to learn something new
- ☐ Unfair treatment
- ☐ Perfectionism (our own or someone else's)
- ☐ Lack of help

THE DISCUSSION

QUESTION 1: Are your top-three discouragers things that come from outside or inside yourself? Share with the group what you discovered about yourself in this exercise.

Keep these factors in mind as we go through today's lesson, and see how you can develop perseverance in the face of the things that are most discouraging to you.

_____

_____

_____

_____

THIS WEEK'S MEMORY VERSES:

The Bible is full of verses that can help us persevere when we face the discouragers in our lives. Memorize one or both of the following verses, and commit to using it when you need encouragement this week.

> *I do not mean that I am already as God wants me to be. I have not yet reached that goal, but I continue trying to reach it and to make it mine. Christ wants me to do that, which is the reason he made me his.* —*Philippians 3:12 (NCV)*

> *I can do everything through him who gives me strength.* —*Philippians 4:13*

PRAYER: Open in prayer.

PADDLING OUT: HOW DO YOU PERSEVERE?

Game for Adults, Teens, and Children

How well do you exhibit perseverance? It will take a bit of perseverance to complete this word-search challenge. Pair up with a partner and find all the perseverance-related words in the puzzle; then reveal the answer to the question, "How do you persevere?"

LEADER/PARENT: *"*How Do You Persevere?*" Word Search* game sheets are in the Week 3 folder on your **SOUL SURFER** Resource CD. Before you begin the session, print enough game sheets to give one to every two people in your group.

THE FILMS

Watch the first Lesson Three video clip on the **SOUL SURFER** Resource DVD.

First Day of Surfing with One Arm: Against all common sense, Bethany actually wanted to get back to surfing, but she was under strict orders to stay out of the water until her wound was healed. She set the date—Thanksgiving Day! The morning before Thanksgiving, Bethany was unable to wait another day. We see her being reminded to stop and pray before she gets back in the water; then we get to watch what happens next.

Also watch the **SOUL SURFER** movie scene in which Bethany makes breakfast for her family and then gets back in the water.

LEADER/PARENT TIP: See the **SOUL SURFER** Leader's Guide for information on how to watch scenes from the movie **SOUL SURFER**.

In this scene, Bethany is adjusting to a "new normal" by making breakfast for her family. Then, one day early, she announces that she's ready to try surfing again.

SOUL SURFER Quote

"It's the perfect time ... to get back in the water."

— *Bethany to her family*

Bethany grew up with two older, very athletic, competitive brothers. They were happy to allow her to join in some aggressive sports such as roller hockey, soccer, and paintball. They knew she was tough, could take whatever came her way, and wouldn't be a crybaby. That, and her "anything you can do I can do better" attitude contributed to her becoming a very strong athlete and determined competitor.[1]

As we learn more about Bethany Hamilton, we see what a tenacious and focused person she really is. It wasn't long after losing her arm that she made up her mind that she would try to surf again.

QUESTION 2: If you were one of Bethany's friends or her parent, how would you have reacted when you realized she was going to try to surf again? What advice would you have given her?

QUESTION 3: We have already identified Bethany as a determined and focused athlete. What else does Bethany's decision to surf again tell you about the kind of person she is? How do you think those characteristics help her, or anyone, be successful in life?

Alternate wording for younger children: Bethany made up her mind that she would try to surf again. Why do you think this was so important to her?

[1] George W. Bush, *Decision Points* (New York: Crown, 2010) 8.

Read 1 Corinthians 9:24-27.

Do you not know that in a race all the runners run, but only one gets the prize? Run in such a way as to get the prize. Everyone who competes in the games goes into strict training. They do it to get a crown that will not last; but we do it to get a crown that will last forever. Therefore I do not run like a man running aimlessly; I do not fight like a man beating the air. No, I beat my body and make it my slave so that after I have preached to others, I myself will not be disqualified for the prize.
— 1 Corinthians 9:24-27

Alternate translation for younger children:

You've all been to the stadium and seen the athletes race. Everyone runs; one wins. Run to win. All good athletes train hard. They do it for a gold medal that tarnishes and fades. You're after one that's gold eternally. I don't know about you, but I'm running hard for the finish line. I'm giving it everything I've got. No sloppy living for me! I'm staying alert and in top condition. I'm not going to get caught napping, telling everyone else all about it and then missing out myself. — 1 Corinthians 9:24-27 (MSG)

QUESTION 4: In this passage, the Apostle Paul compares his commitment to Christ with the commitment of an athlete training for a competition. From what you have learned about Bethany so far, how do you think she measures up to this verse, both as an athlete and in her commitment to Christ?

Alternate wording for younger children: Just as a runner who competes in a race needs to work hard to stay in shape, the Apostle Paul says his life in Jesus takes hard work to stay focused (working on one thing only) and do well. How hard do you think Bethany worked to surf again and why do you think she tried so hard?

QUESTION 5: Fear of failure could have kept Bethany from achieving her dreams. Why do you think Bethany was able to push past her fear and keep working to achieve her dream? Read the quote from George W. Bush below for some insight.

When you know you have unconditional love, there is no point in rebellion and no need to fear failure.[2]

—*George W. Bush, speaking about his parents' love for him*

Alternate wording for younger children: *When you are trying to do something hard, how does it help you to know your parents will love you no matter if you do it or not? What about if you also know God loves you no matter what?*

Read Philippians 3:12-14.

> *I do not mean that I am already as God wants me to be. I have not yet reached that goal, but I continue trying to reach it and to make it mine. Christ wants me to do that, which is the reason he made me his. Brothers and sisters, I know that I have not yet reached that goal, but there is one thing I always do. Forgetting the past and straining toward what is ahead, I keep trying to reach the goal and get the prize for which God called me through Christ to the life above.* —*Philippians 3:12-14 (NCV)*

QUESTION 6: What are some of the goals you have for your life? List a few goals you have for your career, a hobby or sport, your spiritual growth, and making an impact on the lives of others. After reading Philippians 3:12-14, what are some things you need to do to reach your goals?

Alternate wording for younger children: *Think about a time you tried to do something hard and you couldn't do it. If you keep remembering how you couldn't do it, does it make it harder to try again? What can you do to make it easier to try again?*

[2] George W. Bush, *Decision Points* (New York: Crown, 2010) 8.

QUESTION 7: When Paul talks about "forgetting the past," do you think he is talking about forgetting past failures or past successes? Which is more likely to be discouraging when trying to reach a goal?

Alternate wording for younger children: Now, think about a time you worked hard and did something great. Can you think of a reason why remembering that could make you feel like not trying anymore?

THE FILMS

Watch the second Lesson Three video clip on the *SOUL SURFER* Resource DVD.

Adjusting to One Arm: In the days and weeks following the shark attack, Bethany had to face her many losses. Bethany faced an unknown future as well as the feeling she was no longer "normal" or beautiful. Yet, she demonstrates a remarkably positive attitude, trying things on her own before asking for help and refusing to call her condition a handicap.

Also watch the *SOUL SURFER* movie scene in which Bethany learns about Venus de Milo.

LEADER/PARENT TIP: See the *SOUL SURFER* Leader's Guide for information on how to watch scenes from the movie *SOUL SURFER*.

In this scene, Bethany's mom, Cheri, encourages her by showing her an image of the Venus de Milo and giving her a different perspective on beauty.

SOUL SURFER Quote

"For centuries, all around the world, she was considered the pinnacle of beauty, and she has one less arm than you."

— Cheri Hamilton to Bethany

THE DISCUSSION

Before the accident Bethany had a firm spiritual foundation. In her book, *Soul Surfer*, Bethany shares some of her young childhood memories of hearing the Bible read at home and of talking with her parents about the stories and people of the Bible. She also shares about really believing in God, putting your faith in Him, and having a real personal relationship with Him—a bond that's as unique as a fingerprint. Bethany remembers putting her trust in Christ when she was only five years old. She says, "I know that's pretty rare—and I'm not embarrassed. Being tight with God is even more important to me than surfing."[3]

About two weeks before the attack, Bethany and her mom had begun praying every day that God would show them what Bethany was supposed to do with her life. She was committed to hearing from God and following His plans for her, and at that time the issue seemed to take on an urgency that she came to understand later.

Read Matthew 7:24-27.

> **"These words I speak to you are not incidental additions to your life, homeowner improvements to your standard of living. They are foundational words, words to build a life on. If you work these words into your life, you are like a smart carpenter who built his house on solid rock. Rain poured down, the river flooded, a tornado hit—but nothing moved that house. It was fixed to the rock. But if you just use my words in Bible studies and don't work them into your life, you are like a stupid carpenter who built his house on the sandy beach. When a storm rolled in and the waves came up, it collapsed like a house of cards."** —Matthew 7:24-27 (MSG)

QUESTION 8: Bethany and her mom had been praying earnestly about what God wanted to do with her life. Then the impact zone hit. Drawing parallels between Bethany's story and Matthew 7:24-27, what

[3] Bethany Hamilton, *Soul Surfer* (New York: Simon & Schuster, 2004) 133-134.

effect did the shark attack have on Bethany's relationship with God? How, if at all, did it change what she thought about what God may have wanted to do with her life?

Alternate wording for younger children: How important do you think Bethany thought it was to build her life on God's plans for her and her relationship with Him?

 **PROVING THE NAYSAYERS WRONG**

The illustration for this lesson is the true story of a man who needs perseverance just to make it through a day, much less to accomplish all he has done. As you read about Bill Porter's life, imagine what it would take to face his daily struggles, especially if people in your life were trying to discourage you from even trying.

Bill Porter's story is a well-documented public record that has even been turned into a Turner Network Television film called *Door to Door*, starring Oscar®-nominated actor William H. Macy. It's all about proving naysayers wrong. Crippled with cerebral palsy, Bill was told that because of his condition, he would never be able to hold a job. Nevertheless, he secured a sales territory in Portland, Oregon, selling door-to-door for Watkins, best-known for their natural cooking ingredients and home-care products. He was told he wouldn't be able to do all the walking that a door-to-door sales job would require, yet he walked seven to ten miles a day for over thirty years. He was told it would be too difficult to deliver the products with no car, but he devised a method to get them delivered. He was told people wouldn't buy from him because they would be afraid of him or wouldn't be able to understand his speech, but he has collected several awards from Watkins for being top salesman of the year. His is a story of persistence in the face of cruel ridicule from bullies, having his products stolen from him because he couldn't defend himself, repeated injuries from falling because of his medical condition, constant wracking pain, walking for miles out in the harsh Oregon weather, and difficulties with simple things like writing up an order, communicating on the phone, and getting people to trust him enough to open their doors to him. He was determined to succeed, no matter how many times people pointed out his problems. Today, at age seventy-six, he runs a successful website business, still selling Watkins products. In 1997 he was given "America's Award," honoring unsung heroes who personify the American character and spirit.

THE DISCUSSION

Bill Porter is an inspiring example of perseverance. If he had listened to the well-meaning people in his life who were trying to keep him from being hurt or disappointed, he would have never experienced the satisfaction and rewards of success. If he had given up when hurtful people or painful circumstances made his difficulties even harder to surmount, his story would have been quite different, and quite uninspiring.

Read Hebrews 12:1-3.

> *Therefore, since we are surrounded by such a great cloud of witnesses, let us throw off everything that **hinders** and the sin that so easily entangles, and let us run with perseverance the race marked out for us. Let us fix our eyes on Jesus, the author and perfecter of our faith, who for the joy set before him endured the cross, scorning its shame, and sat down at the right hand of the throne of God. Consider him who endured such **opposition** from sinful men, so that you will not grow weary and lose heart.* —Hebrews 12:1-3 (Emphasis added)

QUESTION 9: This passage talks about two types of problems that require perseverance to overcome: hindrances and opposition. The first problem is found in Hebrews 12:1, which tells us to "throw off everything that hinders" so we can run with perseverance. The hindrances in Bill Porter's life were many and obvious—disabilities, injuries, setbacks. What are some of the hindrances that tie you down and entangle you? (If you need to jog your memory about specific things that hinder you, go back and review your answers in the *Checking the Waves* checklist.)

Alternate wording for younger children: When runners race, what kinds of problems could they have? What does it take for them to cross the finish line?

QUESTION 10: What does verse 2 say was Jesus' reason for exhibiting endurance? What good and joyful things has God placed in your life — both now and for the future? How can the thought of those blessings and promises from God help you persevere?

Alternate wording for younger children: When you have something joyful to look forward to, how does it help you do something hard now?

QUESTION 11: The second type of problem mentioned in Hebrews 12:1-3 is opposition. Bill Porter faced opposition in the form of bullies and naysayers in his life. Jesus also faced fierce opposition, as explained in Hebrews 12:2-3. How exactly do we "fix our eyes on Jesus"? What does verse 3 say is the benefit of doing so?

Alternate wording for younger children: When racers keep looking at the finish line, it helps them keep going. How do you think it feels to run a long race, like a marathon, when you can't see the finish line for most of the race? Can you think of a time in your life like that, when you felt like giving up because you didn't think you'd ever finish something? How did you keep going?

Read James 1:2-4.

> *Consider it pure joy, my brothers, whenever you face trials of many kinds, because you know that the testing of your faith develops perseverance. Perseverance must finish its work so that you may be mature and complete, not lacking anything.*
> —James 1:2-4

QUESTION 12: What does James 1:2-4 tell us about the importance of persevering—not giving up? What good results come from persevering? Think of a time in your life when you persevered through a trial. What did you learn from that experience, and how did it change you?

Alternate wording for younger children: Why do you think God wants us to learn to not give up?

_____

_____

_____

_____

_____

THE REFLECTION

Pick one of the three questions below. Take a few moments and think carefully about the question before you answer.

- What was the most important thing you learned from this week's lesson?

- Review the answers you gave in the *Catching the Waves* section. Did the lesson give you insights into ways to overcome the discouragers in your life? If so, what specific concepts or ideas were most helpful to you?

- In what areas do you hope to improve your perseverance because of this lesson?

_____

_____

Reread James 1:2-4.

REFLECTION QUESTION: What is the most difficult issue in your life right now? Describe it in the space below. If you were to look at that trial from God's perspective and consider how He can use it to build perseverance in your life, what might happen? "Consider" means that you are deliberately deciding to view the trial in a joyful way; it doesn't mean the trial is easy or that God doesn't understand your pain or frustration. How can you view that trial as joy and look for God's purpose in it?

Review the Memory Verse: Read the memory verses for this week again (Philippians 3:12, Philippians 4:13), choose the one you want to learn, and commit it to memory by next week's meeting.

Prayer Requests: Before closing your time together, have each member of your group or family share at least one prayer request.

PRAYER: Close in prayer.

Catching the Ride of Your Life

EMBRACE GOD'S PLAN FOR YOU.

CATCHING THE RIDE OF YOUR LIFE

What do roller coasters, motorcycles, mountain bikes, bungee cords, and surfboards all have in common? They have all given people the ride of their lives. Extreme-sports athletes and recreation enthusiasts the world over are seeking the ultimate thrill, the white-knuckled-barely-under-control adventure. With one exception, these exhilarating pastimes take place on equipment that is controlled and operated by humans. Roller coasters start and stop at the control of the operator. Motorcycles slow down and speed up with the grip of the rider. Mountain bikes are directed down treacherous terrain by daredevils. And bungee cords! Silly humans plunge headlong off tall structures, trusting in the elasticity and grip of the cord to pluck them from disaster.

The surfboard follows no such pattern. To catch the ride of your life on a surfboard is to throw yourself upon the mercy of an uncontrollable wave. There is no exerting of influence on the wave, no braking, no accelerating, no turning on or off. Seriously dedicated surfers will sit sometimes for hours, bobbing on the ocean, watching and waiting for the next great wave. They can't control when it surges, but they have to be ready for it when it does. There is something special that surfers experience that most other extreme athletes don't, and that is the exhilaration of joining with the forces of nature for a ride powered by a wave they can't possibly control and could never generate on their own. That's what surfers mean by the ride of your life.

In spiritual terms, the ride of your life refers to a powerful movement of God that carries you along, engaging your life completely, beyond your ability to control it and bigger than you ever imagined. The thrill of riding God's wave is like touching eternity here on earth. There is nothing more exciting than sensing you're a part of something that has the potential of turning the tide of someone's life to become all God intends them to be. When you get to be a part of that kind of holy moment, you realize you're a bit like a surfboard—a powerless piece of fiberglass that can do nothing apart from the wave that gives it its speed, direction, and force.

In this lesson, we will look at how God is using Bethany's return to surfing to give her a platform for His purposes. And we will see her riding the waves God stirs up to meet the needs of people around the world. God helps Bethany discover how He intends to work through her in ways that are unexpected, bigger than she imagined, beyond her control, and thrilling beyond belief.

CHECKING THE WAVES

This Activity Is for Adults and Teens

People talk all the time about discovering God's plan for their lives; but how do you go about doing that? This week, in the *Checking the Waves* activity, we will see that the revelation of our purpose is not an event, but a process God takes everyone through. Author Katie Brazelton is a specialist in the area of life purpose, and in her book *Conversations on Purpose for Women*, she observes that there are typically eight phases of discovering our life purpose, and those phases are revealed in a slowly unfolding revelation from God. She explains that most of us do not have a "blinding revelation" of our purpose as did Saul before he became Paul. Instead, God gives us a series of sneak previews about our destiny, and then at some point we receive a clarifying epiphany about the purpose God has prepared for us.

EIGHT PHASES OF GOD'S REVELATION OF OUR LIFE PURPOSE[1]

Check the phase that best represents where you are currently on your discovery of your life purpose. If you are in between two phases, put an X to mark that spot.

☐ **Calling**   A vague, passionate ache that hovers in your soul as an impression; sneak previews

☐ **Hoping**   A whispered prayer accepting the call, hoping that you've heard right

☐ **Doubting**   A serious confusion and questioning

☐ **Believing**   A knowing, a revelation, an epiphany

☐ **Doing**   A beginning of countless action steps

☐ **Waiting**   A severe test of patience

☐ **Expecting**   A confidence in God's miraculous power

☐ **Birthing**   A precious gifting of His promise

---

[1] Katie Brazelton. *Conversations on Purpose for Women.* (Grand Rapids: Zondervan, 2005).

THE DISCUSSION

QUESTION 1: Even though we might not always be paying attention, God is speaking to us and making His will clear to us. Share with the group how God has spoken to you, and talk about the ways in which you hear from Him.

_____

_____

_____

_____

_____

THIS WEEK'S MEMORY VERSE:

And we know that in all things God works for the good of those who love him, who have been called according to his purpose.
—Romans 8:28

PRAYER: Open in prayer.

PADDLING OUT: TRUST WALK

Game for Adults, Teens, and Children

God asks us to trust Him as we discover our purpose in life. The best way to understand trust is to experience it. Go on a trust walk, where you can't see a thing and follow your guide's leading to get to your purpose.

LEADER/PARENT: Find instructions for "Trust Walk" in the Lesson Four folder on your **SOUL SURFER** Resource CD. Before you begin the session, have blindfolds ready for group participants.

THE FILMS

Watch the first Lesson Four video clip on the *SOUL SURFER* Resource DVD.

Worldwide Mission Opportunities: Bethany now has the opportunity to travel the world, teaming up with World Vision to use what happened to her to help and encourage other people in other cultures. She is especially drawn to those who suffer, and they are drawn to her as well.

LEADER/PARENT NOTE: World Vision is a Christian relief, development, and advocacy organization dedicated to working with children, families, and communities to overcome poverty and injustice. You can visit them at WorldVision.org.

Also watch the *SOUL SURFER* movie scene in which Bethany ministers to the children in Thailand by helping them get back in the water.

LEADER/PARENT TIP: See the *SOUL SURFER* Leader's Guide for information on how to watch scenes from the movie *SOUL SURFER*.

When Bethany arrives in Thailand, the suffering caused by the recent tsunami gives her a different perspective on her own trials. Bethany uses her experiences and love for the ocean to encourage the children to get back in the water.

SOUL SURFER Quote

"Who would have thought that teaching a kid to surf would teach me that surfing isn't the most important thing in the world, and that something else is: love—bigger than any tidal wave, more powerful than any fear."

— *Bethany*

THE DISCUSSION

Read Romans 15:1-2.

> *Those of us who are strong and able in the faith need to step in and lend a hand to those who falter, and not just do what is most convenient for us. Strength is for service, not status. Each one of us needs to look after the good of the people around us, asking ourselves, "How can I help?"* —Romans 15:1-2 (MSG)

QUESTION 2: In your own words, summarize the Apostle Paul's instructions to us in Romans 15:1-2. List them here so you can refer back to them. How can we follow those instructions today?

Alternate wording for younger children: From Romans 15:1-2, what do you think is the most important thing God wants us to do?

QUESTION 3: What does Paul say is the reason God makes us strong? See Romans 15:1-2 above. How do you typically spend your strength each day?

BRAINSTORMING SESSION

Talk with your group about some service projects you might be able to do together to meet the needs of some less-fortunate people near where you live. Discuss whether participating in a short-term mission trip like Bethany's youth group did might be something you can do.

Read 2 Corinthians 1:3-4.

> *Praise be to the God and Father of our Lord Jesus Christ, the Father of compassion and the God of all comfort, who comforts us in all our troubles, so that we can comfort those in any trouble with the comfort we ourselves have received from God.*
> — *2 Corinthians 1:3-4*

QUESTION 4: Underline words and phrases in the passage that describe specific things about God. What do you learn about God in these verses?

QUESTION 5: According to 2 Corinthians 1:4 above, what is one of the reasons God comforts us? How should we respond to God's comfort?

QUESTION 6: One of the turning points in Bethany's life was when she went on her first mission trip, to help in Thailand after the 2004 tsunami. She was moved with compassion toward those who had suffered so much, and when she began to comprehend the enormity of what the Thai people had lost, she began to rethink her own losses with a new perspective. Based on 2 Corinthians 1:3-4, what do you think God was showing Bethany about His will for her life?

Alternate wording for younger children: *Bethany cried when she saw how hurt the people in Thailand were. How do you think God wants to work through Bethany?*

THE FILMS

Watch the second Lesson Four video clip on the *SOUL SURFER* Resource DVD.

Living in God's Purpose and Plan: Bethany is thrust onto the world stage, taking part in media appearances and winning awards that gain her worldwide attention. Making speeches and giving interviews in places where there are no waves is definitely outside of Bethany's comfort zone, but she sees it as a chance to give people hope for their lives. She quotes our *Memory Verse*, Romans 8:28, as the reason God let all this happen to her, which she calls a "blessing in disguise."

THE DISCUSSION

Read 2 Thessalonians 1:11-12.

> **With this in mind, we constantly pray for you, that our God may count you worthy of his calling, and that by his power he may fulfill every good purpose of yours and every act prompted by your faith. We pray this so that the name of our Lord Jesus may be glorified in you, and you in him, according to the grace of our God and the Lord Jesus Christ.** —*2 Thessalonians 1:11-12*

QUESTION 7: What do you think Paul meant in verse 11 when he prayed, "That our God may count you worthy of his calling?" From what you have seen of Bethany and what you have learned about her, do you think God finds her worthy of her calling? Why or why not? Use 2 Thessalonians 1:11-12 for help.

Alternate wording for younger children: To glorify God means to give Him honor and credit for who He is and what He has done. How do you see Bethany bringing glory to God?

_____

_____

_____

QUESTION 8: From 2 Thessalonians 1:11-12, what would you say is our general purpose in life? Look back at your answer in the Checking the Waves activity. How does knowing your general purpose affect your process of discovering God's specific plan for your life?

Alternate wording for younger children: What are some ways you can glorify God (give Him honor) at school and at home?

_____

_____

_____

_____

THE ILLUSTRATION   PAUL'S BLINDING REVELATION

Perhaps the only person to receive a literally "blinding revelation" about their life purpose was the Apostle Paul. This Illustration recalls that dramatic moment and shows us through Paul's example the power of a life fully committed to the Lord Jesus Christ.

Other than Jesus, it can safely be said that the Apostle Paul (formerly called Saul of Tarsus) influenced Christianity more than anyone else.

Before he became a believer in Jesus Christ, Saul was a devoted Pharisee and a determined persecutor of those who followed Christ. Saul approved and watched as the Jews stoned to death Stephen, one of the early church leaders. After Stephen's stoning, many believers fled from Jerusalem, taking with them the Good News about Jesus Christ and spreading that message everywhere they went. Saul began to hunt down the Christians who fled from Jerusalem, round them up, and take them as prisoners back to Jerusalem (Acts 9:1-2).

While Saul was on his way to Damascus, pursuing more Christian refugees, he was struck blind by a bright light. It was the Lord Jesus himself, who stunned Saul when He revealed that He was the one whom Saul was actually persecuting. After being healed of his blindness and filled with the Holy Spirit, Saul shocked the terrified believers by preaching in the synagogue (the Jewish place of worship) and teaching that Jesus is the Son of God. It took a lot of convincing to persuade people that Saul was a genuine convert, but he persisted and grew more and more influential as he proved to peasants, priests, and kings that Jesus is the Christ (Acts 9:20-22).

God called Saul (later called Paul in Acts 13:9) to take the Good News about Jesus to the Gentiles; he was the first disciple to obey Jesus' command to take the gospel to all people. Because Paul was so intelligent and knew the Scriptures so well, he was a powerful evangelist. He also started many churches as he traveled where God's Spirit directed him. Paul endured unimaginable persecution and hardship, including being beaten, arrested, and thrown in prison multiple times.

During his travels and his imprisonments, Paul wrote thirteen letters that make up much of the New Testament of the Bible. From his life we learn that God uses people who obey Him with their whole heart. Paul is our example of spreading the Good News about Jesus. Beside all that, Paul is one of the greatest examples of the power of God to transform and empower the lives of a people who love Him with all their hearts and serve Him with all their strength. Paul was fully committed to God's calling on his life, and nothing stopped him from fulfilling that call from the moment of his conversion to the day he died.

THE DISCUSSION

QUESTION 9: After learning about Bethany's life and reading *The Illustration* of Paul's life, how do you think knowing God's purpose for them influenced their life choices? Knowing what you do now, how important is it for you to discover God's purpose for your life?

Alternate wording for younger children: Why did Paul keep telling people about Jesus even when it got so hard?

QUESTION 10: Even though it would seem that two people like the Apostle Paul and teenager Bethany Hamilton couldn't be more different from each other, see how many similarities you can discover between Paul and Bethany and list them below. In what ways are they different from each other? (If you need a little help, read 2 Corinthians 11:22-27 and Philippians 3:4-11 for information on the life of the Apostle Paul.)

SIMILARITIES

Both loved God from their youth.

_____

_____

_____

_____

_____

_____

_____

DIFFERENCES

_____

_____

_____

_____

_____

_____

_____

Read 2 Thessalonians 1:11-12 again.

> *With this in mind, we constantly pray for you, that our God may count you worthy of his calling, and that by his power he may fulfill every good purpose of yours and every act prompted by your faith. We pray this so that the name of our Lord Jesus may be glorified in you, and you in him, according to the grace of our God and the Lord Jesus Christ.* —2 Thessalonians 1:11-12

QUESTION 11: In what ways will Paul and Bethany go down in history as people who brought glory to God by sharing Christ with everyone they could? How do you think you can bring glory to God?

Alternate wording for younger children: Since bringing glory to God means to honor Him and share the good things He does for us, how can you give glory to God?

Read our Memory Verse, Romans 8:28.

> **And we know that in all things God works for the good of those who love him, who have been called according to his purpose.**
> — Romans 8:28

QUESTION 12: Bethany quoted our *Memory Verse*, Romans 8:28, saying that God was working to bring good out of what happened to her. How do you see this verse working as you are on your own journey toward being "called according to His purpose"?

Alternate wording for younger children: If God can make ALL things work for good, how can He turn a bad thing into a good thing?

With a big smile, Bethany said, "Having one arm is how He uses me. God put me on this earth to serve Him. I'm still happy."

THE REFLECTION

Pick one of the three questions below. Take a few moments and think carefully about the question before you answer.

- **What was the most important thing you learned from this week's lesson?**

- **Review your answer in the Checking the Waves section. What have you learned, if anything, about discovering God's purpose for your life?**

- **In what ways do you hope to bring glory to God with your life?**

Reread 2 Corinthians 1:3-4.

REFLECTION QUESTION: Below, write down some of the trials you have been through in your life. How has God comforted you in those trials, and what have you learned from them? The Bible teaches us that we can take some of the most difficult experiences in our life and use them to comfort people in similar circumstances. Bethany applied what she learned from the shark attack when she comforted the children in Thailand. How, specifically, could you take your trials and experiences and use them to minister to others?

Review the Memory Verse: Read the memory verse for this week again (Romans 8:28) and commit it to memory as an encouragement that you are able to accomplish whatever God calls you to do.

Prayer Requests: Before closing your time together, have each member of your group or family share at least one prayer request.

PRAYER: Close in prayer.

SOUL SURFER DVD-based Study
Be inspired by this four-week study featuring exclusive video of Bethany Hamilton.

This four-week DVD-based study includes a resource DVD with *Heart of a Soul Surfer*—a thirty-minute documentary with interviews—and exclusive surfing and family footage of Bethany Hamilton before and after the shark attack. *Heart of a Soul Surfer* digs deep into the heart of Bethany's unwavering faith in God and provides video clips to support the four-week study.

With its encouraging portrayal of family values and its uplifting message, the *SOUL SURFER* DVD-based Study will resonate with adults, families, and teens alike!

The kit includes:

- *Heart of a Soul Surfer* documentary plus clips for four weekly lessons
- A *SOUL SURFER* Study Guide
- A leader's guide with instructions for small group leaders, parents, and youth leaders

Look for the *SOUL SURFER* **DVD-based Study** at your local Christian bookstore or visit **Outreach.com** for bulk quantities.

SOUL SURFER: Catching God's Wave for Your Life
An inspirational book for preteens and teens

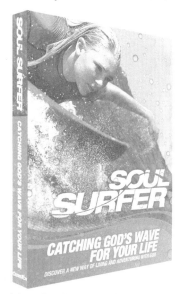

Soul Surfer: Catching God's Wave for Your Life will both encourage and challenge preteens and teens through the incredible true story and example of teen surfer Bethany Hamilton. Through the uplifting message of this book, readers will:

· Be challenged to gain a greater perspective on life

· Believe God loves them and has a good plan for their lives

· Be inspired to persevere and not give up when things get tough

· Be faithful and develop a grateful heart

· Be encouraged to embrace God's dream for their lives

Help your teen discover a new way of living and adventuring with God!

Look for **SOUL SURFER: Catching God's Wave for Your Life** at your local Christian bookstore or visit **Outreach.com** for bulk quantities.

Heart of a Soul Surfer
The powerful, inspirational story of Bethany Hamilton on DVD!

Special Edition DVD includes:

- Widescreen Format
- Subtitles in 9 Languages
- New Bonus Videos
  "Day in the Life"
  "Surf Training with Bethany"
  "Gospel Presentation"
- Free 13 x 9 Poster of Bethany

Heart of a Soul Surfer: The Bethany Hamilton Documentary offers her family's perspective on the true story and life of a promising young surfer who discovered her purpose in life as she overcame the loss of her arm to a fourteen-foot tiger shark in 2003.

This thirty-minute, faith-based documentary conveys Bethany's heart and tackles the difficult question, Why does God allow bad things to happen in our lives? Dealing with topics from self-consciousness to courage to faith in God, *Heart of a Soul Surfer* presents an inspiring story and message in a fun, exciting way—told from the heart of a young woman with great passion and dedication to God.

Ask for the Special Edition retail DVD of Heart of a Soul Surfer at your local Christian bookstore or visit HeartofaSoulSurfer.com.